WHY CHESS MATTERS

A Parent and Teacher's Guide to the Ancient Game of Kings

By

Brian Ashley

This book is dedicated to:

My wonderful wife Barbara, who has watched me play endless games of chess, pore through chess literature endlessly, and supported me as I created my chess academies in Sausalito, California and New Smyrna Beach, Florida.

To my children Scott, Noelle, John, Melinda, and Lauren, who have supported me in all I do.

To my grandchildren, Miranda, Madeline, Hannah, Poppy, Statham, Grant, Georgia, Fanny, August, Penny, and Zeke, and my great grandchildren, Wynn, Millie and Bennie.

Author's Note

This book is meant to entertain and inform. It is by no means complete. I would highly recommend that you use internet research to discover more.

Table of Contents

Forward by Ben Herring

I first met Brian Ashley when he approached me about adding chess to our junior golf program at the Golf Club at Venetian Bay. It sounded intriguing so I gave him one hour right before lunch for one day out of our three-day Jr. Golf Summer Camp.

Brian began by giving us a brief overview of the history of chess, its popularity throughout the world, and its astounding number of potential moves. After this surprising and compelling introduction, he proceeded to give us basic instruction on the game of chess. A lot of kids already knew how to play and helped kids who were not familiar with the game. Brian helped everyone as we started playing.

To sum up, the hour was an immense success. The kids loved it as did the parents. Chess is now an important part of our junior golf program, and we have even started an adult chess club.

Chess, like golf, is an excellent tool to help kids learn, grow and to think strategically while building self-esteem and self-confidence. I would highly recommend adding chess to your junior golf program and include chess in your family activities! This book is an excellent place to start.

Ben Herring, PGA Golf Professional

Introduction

I teach chess to kids, mostly ages 6-13, both boys and girls. I like to see them sitting across from one another in quiet concentration, smiling and well-mannered, with an appropriate competitive mind-set, rather than staring and interacting with a screen. It got me thinking how beneficial it would be if parents could discover the positive influence chess can have on their kids, and that is how *Why Chess Matters* was born.

This book has been written with educators and parents in mind who wish to approach child education with more creative methods than before. Therefore, this is more than a book about chess; it is an additional tool to help you be a more complete parent, teacher, and coach. The objectives below outline what I hope you will take from this book and then apply these newly learned skills to your parenting, teaching or coaching.

Objective number one: to convince you that chess is worthy of its reputation. That is, it is a far-reaching and historic game of noble proportions, enjoyed in every civilized culture across the world. Chess transcends differences in language, customs, culture, age, and gender. Chess can be played by anyone, regardless of culture, location, or language. All you need is a chess board and an eagerness to learn.

Objective number two: it will make you a better parent or teacher. It will give you certain skills and insights which non-chess playing parents do not possess. You do not have to be good at the game. What is required is a basic understanding of the principles of the game, which you will acquire from this book.

Objective number three: the bond with your child will improve and endure as a result of you playing chess together. Perhaps surprisingly, chess can be much more meaningful than other games. Chess is a metaphor for life, and you can use this insight to help kids with various questions, issues, or concerns. This all transpires from the richness of the game itself. You and your child will become accustomed to being with one another, sharing thoughts and new ideas on the game of chess, and eventually the game of life.

Objective number four: add a family activity. If not already done, select one night a week for "Family Night." Family Night has three parts: Part one is to instruct the kids about something not learned in school. For example, "What's a bank account?" or "How many different types of jobs are there?," or something else unusually interesting. Part two is to provide the opportunity to be creative with something like drawing, painting, or even story writing or storytelling. Part three, is game time with chess being the game of choice (Call it "chess time?"). Kids love games and they love to play games with their parents. For as serious and far-reaching as is the nature of chess, there is one underlying persistent fact: playing chess is fun!

Objective number five: to make chess an important part of a child's educational experience with you as the guide, advisor and practice opponent. As you read about the educational power of chess, you will wonder why it isn't part of every elementary school's curriculum. Chess teaches things that regular schools don't, but a child needs a savvy teacher (you!) to guide him or her.

My hope is that this book will convince you to get enthused about learning, using chess as the tool. If you are a parent, aunt, uncle, or grandparent, you have the opportunity with the game of chess to have lifelong interaction with your child, niece, nephew or grandchild.

If you are an educator, a business strategist, coach or consultant, herein are many ideas which can serve as a template for success.

Brian Ashley
November 2023
New Smyrna Beach, Florida

PART I: The Game of Kings

When I founded the Sausalito Chess Academy twenty years ago, I started taking chess more seriously. Discovering my curiosity alive and well, I started asking *why* questions and the one most puzzling was, *"Why are none of my games alike?"* They might be vaguely similar, but never identical.

Awestruck

Reflecting on my many games of chess, when I was first learning at age 8, my teacher who was my nine-year-old friend at the time, showed me a win called, "Fool's Mate". This move can easily be repeated, especially by beginners. But other than that, once you get a few moves into a game, no two games are exactly alike. I play several times a day now, and estimate that since I got back into it, I've played between 50,000 and 100,000 games. Surely it must be a vast coincidence that no two games are alike. Well, it isn't, and here is why.

Back in the 1950's, a professor named Shannon was pondering almost the same thing. He wondered how computers would perform when mathematics were applied to the game. A computer can play at the speed of light, so we could create a machine that could go through all the moves available, do that in an instant and come up with the next move. He started with, "How many possible games of chess are there?" The answer: 10 to the 120th power, or 10

11

followed by 1 20 zeros! This initial estimate was astonishing. That number is so big it would take more seconds than ever existed, and more seconds projected into the imaginary future to finally come up with the next move!

To give you an idea how big all this is, try these comparisons out for size.

- ✓ The atoms in the visible universe: 10 to the 80th power! (80 zeros)

- ✓ The number of grains of sand on every beach in the world: 10 the 27th power! (27 zeros)

- ✓ The number of stars in the entire universe: 10 to the 24th power! (24 zeros)

The computer would *never* make a move! There isn't enough time, real or imagined!

Professor Shannon, for all his efforts, got his glory. They decided to call his number, "Shannon's Number." (Wow. How original.)

Thoughts on Learning How to Learn

Although this is a book that demonstrates the impact of chess on the world, just as importantly it is a book about *learning.*

In the last century, a famous educator named Benjamin Bloom, laid out a hierarchy of learning in three domains: cognitive, affective, psychomotor. The cognitive domain has rightly dominated the educational landscape

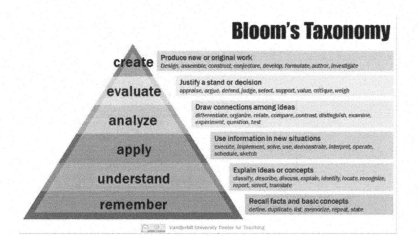

since its inception because it neatly describes and explains that learning is a structure. It occurs in a hierarchy, with very specific experiences and achievements at each level. He published three charts called "Bloom's Taxonomy." The chart of the cognitive domain is shown here.[1] Note that he traces the simplistic to the artistic; from remembering and regurgitation all the way up to original creativity. Note that in between these poles are a wealth of activities, an accumulation of knowledge and skill refinement.

---

[1] Courtesy of Vanderbilt U. Center for Teaching

In the spirit of Bloom's Taxonomy, I've created a chess taxonomy that shows what happens when you learn chess.

Skills	Chess Example	Personal Action
ASHLEY'S COMPARATIVE LEARNING THEORY & CHESS TAXONOMY		
Assemble, construct, develop, formulate	Great games are original, elegant, surprising, wonderful works of art. You study historical games of famous grandmasters.	You make your own brilliant moves and create your own elegant games.
Appraise, select, support, value, critique	A move is a decision made from appraising the situation and selecting it from many possibilities. It harbors an idea of future scenarios. You expect something to happen because of your or your opponent's decision. You must also deal with unmet expectations if what you anticipated happening doesn't happen. This can involve emotions as well as objective thought, which can be difficult to deal with without the right mindset.	You become skilled in decision-making in the face of seemingly endless choices: Do I trade queens or do something else? Do I sacrifice a knight or a bishop? Do I push my pawn or take a piece? Endgames apprear in a similar fashion as did moves in the previous stage.
Organize, Compare, Contrast, Distinguish, Examine	The board changes when either you or your opponent make a move. In both cases, the new battlefield, the chessboard, needs to be reanalyzed, comparing new positions. From just one move, new threats emerge, new defenses appear and new conclusions must be drawn. The magic of chess is that your next move seems to suddenly appear out of nowhere as you study the board. What was hidden in plain sight becomes hidden no more.	*Non-Cognitive Analytical Skills* develop deep in your neural networks. When playing, moves appear. A move that was previously invisible to you seems to materialize before your eyes. You feel the rush of discovery.
Execute, Implement, Solve, Use	You've learned principles and different special attacks and use them in games. You've both won and lost many games.	You create a fork, pin or double attack.
Explain, Identify, Recognize, Reproduce, Select	You've learned how the pieces move and are successfully able to reproduce them on the board.	You can play a game and win or lose.
Define, Memorize, Repeat	You can explain how the pieces move.	You can show how the pieces move, including castling and en passant.

Let me use learning English as an example. Like you learned letters, then words, then sentences then essays, where you created your own prose, it is possible to learn chess in the same way. Like the first-grade speller that grows up to be a playwright or a novelist, the beginning chess player may grow to be an expert at the game, and perhaps a grandmaster. You learn how to place the pieces on the board, how they move, then how to play, then how to think strategically. From there it will be up to you how far you want to take your newfound skills. At the apex of the chess learning curve, creating loftier games of chess can only be described as elegant works of art or genius.

You may experience the joy of creating your own elegant games as you play more, learn from your experiences and study the game. Additionally, as you gain knowledge and experience, you will encounter, examine and admire well-known games played by legendary grandmasters. The internet makes it easy. It will be the same experience as if you are studying timeless works of art.

The Origins of Chess

Kings of old had an unavoidable pastime: *war.* When they weren't doing battle, they were thinking about it. It is therefore not so surprising that a game of war would spring from the king and his court. War plays out on a battlefield and for this

A Chess Board

purpose a board was created with alternate-colored squares from which an attack could be planned, or a defense set up. On this battlefield, the armies start on each side of the board, facing each other.

In days of old, war was not only carried out by the fighting army, but also with the involvement of support groups like wives, priests, animals, "machinery" and structures. The animals to which I am referring to are horses and elephants. The "machinery" were chariots, and structures were buildings, namely the castle. Therefore, a side consisting of representatives from various roles, some fighting and some not, were created to form "chessmen."

The group of chessmen (the army) consists of the pawns, the minor pieces, and the major pieces.

Here are the members of the "chess army," with two images. One is as they may have looked in real life, and the other is how they look on a chessboard.

The first line is the infantry, or foot soldiers, called *Pawns.*

Behind the line of pawns is an army of varying power.

The calvary, or horsemen, called *Knights,* recalling the powerful horseman who could jump enemy lines and kill almost at will. The Knight is a minor piece.

The clergy, who represent the power of God called *Bishops,* for no army could engage in battle without righteous reasons and God on their side. The Bishop is also a minor piece.

17

In the early centuries of chess, as it flowed through ancient Persia, chariots were a powerful part of the Persian army, and the  word for chariot in Persian is *Rukh*. So, the Rukh became part of the army of chess. The Rukh is a major piece.

In the middle ages, as the game worked its way across various cultures in Europe, the image of the chariot was replaced with the image of a castle. In Medieval Europe, around 1000 AD,  castles were easier to understand and remember than chariots, since castles were all over the place, and chariots were but a distant memory from ancient times. Although the piece changed into a *Castle*, the name "rukh" stuck, and it eventually morphed into the spelling we have today, *Rook*. However, the name "castle" didn't entirely disappear and many chess books show that you can interchange the words "Rook" or "Castle." One of the moves that you will soon learn that involves the Rook, is called "Castling," not "Rooking."

And what King in his right mind would go to war without the blessing of arguably the most powerful person in the kingdom, *The Queen.*[2] She is a major piece.

And finally, we meet the feeble *King,* whose "life" is at stake in the war, and the capturing of

whom is the whole point. In the game of chess, he has truly little power until the very end of the game, when the situation is just him and a few Pawns. At that point in the game he becomes very powerful.

King at the Endgame

About a hundred years ago, bowing to women's suffrage, and subtly acknowledging who wears the pants in the kingdom, the word "chessmen" was largely dumped and replaced by the words "chess pieces."

As the game of chess was forming, despite the historic origins of each piece, gamers of old realized that you could not have idle participants. Pieces that just prayed for the army, or who nagged the King, or just stayed in one place and did nothing, were of no use in a new and exciting

---

[2] Those of us who are married would not argue the point!

game of war. So, they gave each piece an active role in the fight.

Since the infantry is the most expendable part of an army, and leads the charge into battle, there are eight Pawns. Lose one or two, no biggie. Since Bishops, Castles, and Knights are much more important than Pawns, there are two of each of those, and they are much more powerful. And as in real life, there is only one King and one Queen, and we've already established who wears the chainmail pants in the kingdom.

Now that you know who's who and their origins, let us take a closer look at the elements of the royal game of chess. In Chapter One we examine the board and the pieces and in Chapter Two, the language of chess called, "notation." In Chapter Three, you will see how to play and learn how to think strategically.

Chapter One: The Board and the Players

With the history lesson over, we can now put it all together and put the pieces on the board to begin a game.

The Board

As previously stated, the chessboard is really a map of the battlefield. It is a simple checkboard of 64 alternating light and dark squares. There are three directions that pieces can take during the game: up and down along the columns, right and left along the rows, and diagonally along the same color squares. The columns are referred to as "files," the rows are "ranks," and the diagonals are "diagonals." We will discuss more of this in Chapter 2. To begin a game, you only need to know two things.

1. "White on right" (White square in right corner)

2. Queen on its own color.

21

From there, you set up the rest of the players. The previous image is what the set-up looks like to begin a game.

The Players

Now we will get to know the players in battle. Allow me to introduce the "army" on the board. There are 16 players in this army. The King, the permanent capture of whom is the point of the game, the Queen and two Rooks, called "Major Pieces;" two Knights, and two Bishops, called, "Minor Pieces," and eight Pawns, called well, "Pawns." Historically, one army is Black, and one is White, but over the years, many contrasting colors have been used as well as various themes, like Crusaders vs. Moors, Yanks vs. Rebs, etc.

We will go back and forth from, "chessmen," to "players," to "pieces," despite one noticeably not a man, namely the Queen.

In this image, you see that each piece has value too,

King, Queen, Bishop, Knight, Rook, Pawn
∞   9   3   3   5   1

depending on their power. In chess, the number represents

their value in Pawns.[3] As you may have expected, the Queen is worth 9 Pawns. Next are the Rooks, worth 5 Pawns. Bishops and Knights are worth 3 Pawns, and each Pawn, is valued at one Pawn. You will learn why the power is distributed this way in the next section.

The King is not included in the "value scale," because when you capture the King, the game is over. So you can look at the King like he is worth everything or nothing, depending on your personal preference. At any rate, the King is not part of the Pawn tracking when you are playing a game, because he is never off the board until the game is over. Keeping track of Pawn value captured is not part of the official game but can be helpful for beginners to get a general idea of how they are doing. For example, if I have the value of eighteen Pawns captured, like a Queen(9), two Knights (6), and three Pawns (3), and you have only one Pawn captured, I'm most likely going to win. Although interesting and informative, you can play and enjoy chess while being oblivious to the number value of each piece.

Men in real battles have distinct functions. Infantry charges on foot, the artillery shoot giant bullets from a cannon at long distance, rifleman are medium distance deadly killers with long guns, the calvary on horses armed with swords or lances, etc. They all do "army stuff," like charge,

---

[3] You can say "points" in everyday conversation.

attack, capture, and employ teamwork to triumph. Additionally, they can retreat, escape, get captured, and accidently killed, or in the most noble of causes by sacrificing their life for the greater good. Chess simulates this.

During the game, chessmen may be attacking but they all do it differently due to the way they move. There is a hierarchy of power directly attributable to what each piece can do on the board. So a piece that can move almost anywhere it wants (the Queen), would naturally be more powerful than a piece that can move only one square at a time as a Pawn does, for example.

Let us now turn to the powers and abilities of individual pieces and Pawns in our army and you will learn how each one moves.

Please note, there is a universal unwritten rule, when showing a chess game on a printed page in a learning situation, white is always on the bottom of the board and black is on the top. That is, white is on ranks one and two, and black is on ranks seven and eight at the beginning of the game. Looking at the board on any of these pages, white is attacking up and black is attacking down.

The Queen

The Queen is the most powerful piece on the board. She can move in a straight line and in any direction for as many squares as is open. Since she is so powerful, she is usually the center of attention. But I caution beginners to try to not rely

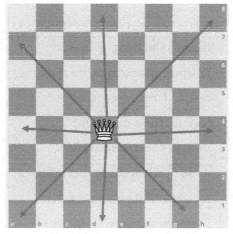

How the Queen Moves

on her too much. She's powerful, not invincible. Like other pieces and Pawns, she can be captured. This makes a Queen sacrifice one of the most dramatic moves in chess.

The Rooks

The next most powerful pieces are the Rooks. They move along files or ranks for as many squares as you want or are available. A good strategy is to let them hang back and control the file.

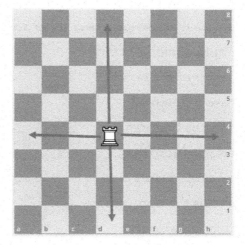

How the Rooks Move

25

The Bishops

The Bishops move diagonally only, with each Bishop staying on its own color. They are powerful too, as they can move across the entire board. The Bishops are the only players that must stay on their own-colored squares.

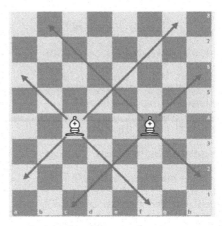

How the Bishops Move

They are called, "The Light Squared Bishop" and "The Dark Squared Bishop."

The Knights

Knights do not move in a straight line and are the only pieces that can jump over other squares, either occupied or empty. Knights in the center of the board have 8 potential squares they can attack. Note that landing squares are always the opposite color on which the Knight sits. During a

How the Knights Move

26

game or when practicing, the following mantras help:

- "Up two, over one."

- "Down two, over one."

- "Left two, up one."

- "Right two, down one."

It means for example, "Move two squares to the right and down one square." Note that for each up, down, left or right move, there are two options. It's best to practice this with random pieces, showing yourself how they can jump and take across the board.

So far, we've talked about pieces that have a lot of "reach." That is they can capture from a long distance. They hide in plain sight, and Bam! It seems that out of nowhere they capture. We now turn our attention to Pawns and the King, who do not have so much reach.

How Pawns Move

The Pawns

On this board, the white Pawns are attacking up and the black Pawns are attacking down. True to the nature of their foot soldier origins, the Pawns can only move forward.

27

For their first move, however, they do have some leeway; they can move either one or two squares, and that is totally up to you. They can capture too, but when they do, it is only on a diagonal. "How Pawns Move" depicts both moves.

The Pawns also have a tricky move called, *"en passant."* Yes, it's French, and it means, "in passing," and originated around 1400 AD. If Pawns cross the middle of the board, white reaching the

En Passant

5th rank and black reaching the 4th, they can take the Pawn in the adjacent file, *if the opposing Pawn tries to pass them.*

Here is the way this unique move works: Look at the white Pawn on d2. He wants to escape being captured by the black Pawn on c4. So, he moves to d4 instead of d3, in order to avoid being captured. But the en passant rule says that if white moves to either d3 or d4, he can be captured either way. In other words, if he does move to d4, it is *as if* he moved to d3. Black takes white and black's new square is d3. It is the same for the black Pawn on f7. If he moves to f6, white can get him. If he moves to f5, with the en passant rule, white can still get him. You only have one chance to do this, and that is on the next move.

Besides this unique move, Pawns have another reward coming to them for service above and beyond the call of duty. No, it is not *Pawn Heaven*, but for you it could be. It's called "Pawn Promotion," and it works like this. If a lowly Pawn reaches the other side of the board, he can be transformed into any player except the King. Ninety nine percent of the time, he is transformed into a Queen, and yes, you can have more than one Queen on the board, and

Former Pawns!

they don't back stab each other, or become jealous and spread rumors about one another, nor do they compete to be the "fairest of them all."

When you promote a Pawn, you now have a one-two Queen punch that is usually unstoppable.

29

The King

Just like in real life, the King lays back and watches his army do its job of attacking the enemy and protecting him while trying to win the war. So, he mostly hides until the end of the game when most of his army has 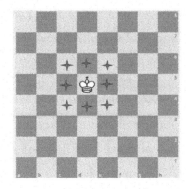 been captured. He can only move one square at a time, but it can be in any direction.

He must follow a couple of rules  though. Opposing Kings must keep at least one square away from each other, and the King can't put himself in check.

One more thing. If he gets into check, he must immediately get out of check on the next move. He can get out of check three ways. One, just move. Two, block the piece that is checking him by moving one of his own pieces between him and the checking piece. And three, capture the attacker.

Sometimes there is an occasion in a game where a move causes the King to be in check from two pieces simultaneously. This is called *double check,* and in this case his only choice is to move.

Now that we've seen how each player moves, we will discuss the language of chess. The language of chess is shorthand for how pieces move, where they are, and recording games for future reproduction.

Chapter Two: Chess Language

A special note here. You don't need to know "chess language" to play the game. Chess language is primarily a way of recording and reproducing games, but it is also a way to describe the action of a game. I went for years as a kid, playing the game for fun, and I didn't know any of this. But I was taught on the streets of New York, face-to-face. That is quite different from reading about chess in a book. It's easier to learn face to face.

In a book you need written language to explain things and in chess it's called "notation," and in *chess notation,* we focus on three things: the squares, the players and what they did. Chess notation tells you what piece is on what square and what action happened.

We begin with the board. Each column is designated by a lower-case letter, a-h, and called a "file." Each row is designated by a number, 1-8 and is called a "rank." Rank number 1 is always at the bottom and is where

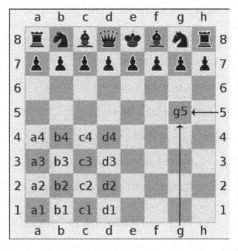

the white pieces begin the game. Rank number 8 is always at the top and is where the black army is placed.

Each square has a "name," and it is where the rank-and-file meet. So, the lower left hand corner square is called, a1. Then moving across in the same row is b1, then c1, etc. all the way to h1. See g5 in the diagram as an example of how squares are named. You don't *need* to know this to play, but it's good to be aware of.

Looking to the next chart, you can see each piece is noted by either a symbol or a capital letter. The one exception is Pawns. They are noted by the square on which they occupy. Symbols are used in books and references to chess games. For this purpose,

Piece	In Person	Symbol	Letter	Pawn Value
King			K	Not Included
Queen			Q	9
Rook			R	5
Bishop			B	3
Knight			N	3
Pawn			No specific name. It is noted by the name of the square it is on.	1

you can get special fonts for printing. When recording a chess game, you would use just the letter and not the symbol.

Chess notation is used in tournaments when you want to record a game or you can reproduce famous games from hundreds of years ago, which is rather cool.

34

The following is an example of notation from one of my online games. The great part of playing online is that the system keeps records for you. You can print it out and reproduce it like I've done here, or you can get a program called PGN. Saving a game as PGN (just like you would save something in word or excel) reproduces your live game!

You can go backward and forward as much as you like, studying your game. Here are the first five moves of one of my online games, demonstrating how chess notation works.

[Date "2021.03.10"]
PuRe2002 (WHITE) V. Edward Book (BLACK)
Edward Book won by checkmate
1. e4... e5

2. f4... exf4

3. Bc4... Nf6

4. Nc3... Be7

5. d4... O-O

6. and so on, until the end of the game.

What follows is each line explained in detail. The top lines show the date, who played, who was white and black, and who won. Each number is a move, and the notation on the left is for white, and on the right, for black. Notice that where a piece ends up is recorded, not where it has been. In number three above, "Bc4," the Bishop is moved to c4 and we know it can only be the white square Bishop[4]. As the game progresses, refer to the previous move to see from what square each piece came.

Here is the notation explained from the first move:

1. e4...e5

White Pawn moves to
Black Pawn moves to e5.

2. **f4... exf4**

White Pawn moves to
f4... Black Pawn on e5,
takes White Pawn on
f4, as shown by the
arrow. The white Pawn
is now captured and off
the board.

---

[4] Sometimes during a game we need to know which Knight we want moved. In this case we note either the rank or the file to: N2d4, or Ned4.

With the white pawn out, the game continues.

3. Bc4...Nf6

   White Bishop to
   c4.... Black Knight
   moves to f6.

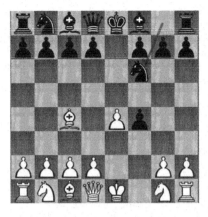

4. Nc3... Be7

   White Knight to c3...
   Black Bishop to e7.

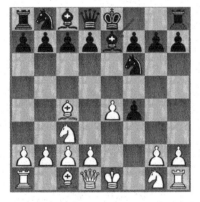

5. d4... 0-0

   White Pawn to d4...
   Black Castles. The
   game ended 18 moves
   later, but now you get
   the idea of notation.

"Castling" is moving your King into castle-like protection. You do it by moving your King two squares toward the Rook, then place the Rook on the inside square next to the King, all in one move. The King is now inside a little protective "castle." You can do it on the Kingside or the Queenside. See the next board.

In this example from another game, White has castled Kingside (0-0), and Black has castled Queenside. (0-0 0)

NOTATION	MOVE
X	Captures
0-0	Kingside Castle
0-0-0	Queenside Castle
"+"	Check
"++"	Checkmate
1-0	White Wins
0-1	Black Wins
1/2	Draw

This is a chart of commonly used notations denoting action, and the last three denote the outcome of a game.

Chapter Three: Playing the Game

Now you know how pieces move and have seen a couple of examples. This part of the book is about learning how to play Chess.

How does a game get started, continue and end? It's as simple as this: white moves first, then black, then white, and so on, until the game is over.

As you are playing, here are some questions that you will ask yourself.

"What piece am I going to move and why?

"What move is my opponent going to make and why?"

"What can I attack?"

"Is something attacking me? Am I in jeopardy somehow?"

"What is that creep thinking now? "(just kidding)

The point is that you are always thinking strategically. You are looking at the whole board and let it speak to you. You try moves. You make good moves and bad, and then react. The game goes on. You never let up. You see openings; you go for the throat! You are attacked! What to do? And so on and so on, and that is chess.

By now you might be thinking this game is too hard and impossible to play. Memorizing how the pieces move is like learning the alphabet in kindergarten, or you might be thinking something like, "I hate mountains! What the heck was I thinking?" as you stare up at Mount Everest.

My advice to you is, don't despair! You are bumping up against some of the first benefits of playing chess: perseverance, practice, how to handle frustration, and what to do if things seem overwhelming! Additionally, as you get to know and experience chess, you will start having fun. At first it will be the fun of capturing pieces and winning. Then you will begin to appreciate higher level attack combinations and you might even look at historic games and appreciate the beauty of a game and the mind of an old chess master. I'm in awe of the insight brought to the game by guys who lived 200 years ago and more recently by the ladies of the chess world. For example, search, "Paul Morphy, Opera Game," and see what you find.

The best way to learn to play and improve is to acquaint yourself with the basic ideas of chess. These ideas are called *Chess Principles*.

Chess Principles

Chess Principles are like rules, and like many rules, good players know when to break them. However, above all, they are historically proven ideas, guidelines, and observations. Thinking is required if you wish to increase your advantage. There are overall guiding principles that apply to any portion of the game, and there are principles that apply to the traditional three game segments: the Opening, the Middle Game, and the Endgame. Principles help you think strategically and productively in any situation. Examples of Opening Principles are, *control the center*, *don't move the same piece twice*, and *don't bring the Queen out too early*.

There is another side to principles too, and that is prevention. If at all possible, while you employ principles to your *advantage*, you want to stop your opponent from applying the principles to his or her game, which keeps them at a *disadvantage*. A fitting example of this is when beginners make the mistake of moving their Queen out too early. They end up having to move their Queen all over the place to avoid getting captured by one piece after another. So while you are developing piece after piece, each attacking the Queen, your opponent is moving the same piece, the Queen, not only twice but many times! At the end of a few moves, they might have the Queen

Black Queen Out Too Early: Disaster!

41

on a safe square, but you have all your pieces developed and have castled to boot, and he has nothing out but his Queen!

We will go over principles in depth as we learn about the Opening, Middle and Endgame. Now that you have been introduced to principles, learning about chess etiquette is in order.

Manners and Sportsmanlike Conduct

Before each game, it is appropriate to begin with a handshake and wish, "Good Luck!" to your opponent in spite of you wanting him to end the game in a whimpering pool of saliva and tears, as you have crushed the life out of him.[5]

After the game, win or lose, and if you are in tears instead, it's still a handshake and "Good Game." (Even while your inner voice is screaming insults at him and calling his mother bad names.)

Parts of the Game

As previously stated, the game is broken down into three segments, *The Opening, The Middle Game* and *The Endgame*, each with guiding principles.

---

[5] Just kidding!

Each part of a chess game is exciting, with literally billions of moves and positions, some powerful and in-your-face, and others very sneaky and subtle. There are entire books devoted to the subtleties of each game segment, and there have been famous players throughout history that have been tagged as excellent in one or another segment.

Games on average are forty moves, but some games are over in four moves and some games have close to a hundred moves. Before we look at each game segment of chess, you might find yourself asking, "Why this move and not some other move?" The short answer is that over the centuries, it has been shown statistically that principles mainly work in favor of winning, and not following them generally favors losing.

If you want a scholarly treatise on the "Why" of chess moves, I recommend buying Irving Chernev's, "Logical Chess, Move by Move/Every Move Explained." This is a terrific book that explains just about everything by studying historically famous games. I also recommend Josh Waitzkin's online Chess Academy found on YouTube.

One other thing. The word, "move" in chess is not exactly synonymous with the word "develop." So the principle, "Develop your Knights before your Bishops," means, "Move your Knights to principle-following squares before moving your Bishops to principle-following squares." If you do this, then you have "well developed minor pieces," If you don't do this, for example, if you move your knight to h3 instead of f3, you have a "poorly developed piece," because you didn't follow the principle, "control the center."

We'll now move on to each game part, the Opening, Middle Game, then Endgame. We start with "The Opening."

The Opening

The first few moves in chess are dedicated to one thought: *control the center of the board*. Chess is a game of choices and consequences, and in the opening, the choices are easy: *move toward the*

center. In this example, move one is correct: e4...e5. Nc8 is incorrect, as it does not effectively help control the center. You'll have to take my word for it regarding the consequences of not doing this in the opening. Or better yet, as you get into the game, try a couple of games where you don't follow this basic principle and see what happens!

44

For the purpose of learning how to begin and what moves to make, this is an imaginary board where white was allowed to move and black wasn't. Note that the center is totally controlled by the Pawns, Knights and Bishops. The blue lines show what Pawns and Bishops control,

Imaginary Opening: Black is frozen

and the splotches show where Knights can land.

On this board, white has castled on the Kingside, the Queen has moved up and out of the way, and the Rooks have "connected," and moved to control the center.

We now leave this imaginary scenario and go back to the real world.

White always moves first, and what follows is a summary of Opening Principles.

1. Control the Center

    a. Move your King's Pawn first, two squares.

    b. Next, move your King's Knight, or if your opponent gives you the move, d4, move your Queen's Pawn out.

    c. Move your Kingside Bishop getting ready to "Castle," but you don't have to Castle on the next move. Sometimes it's ok to wait to see what "develops."

2. Move your Queenside Knight then Queenside Bishop.

3. Don't move the same piece twice.

4. Castle and keep your King's Pawns "still." That is, don't move the Pawns in front of your King. Imagine them this way: Consider the three Pawns a "wall." If you move one of them, you no longer have a wall. You have a picket fence where something can slip through the slats.

5. Don't move your Queen out too early.

46

Checkmate and game over usually occurs well past the opening. However, there is one type of checkmate that occurs in the Opening and that checkmate is called, "Fool's Mate."

There are a few variations of it and it is a fun thing to try. Fool's Mate is a short game of 4 to 6 moves resulting in a checkmate. Every move black makes is a mistake. He doesn't follow the principles. Go online to see more examples.

Fool's Mate

1. E4...f5

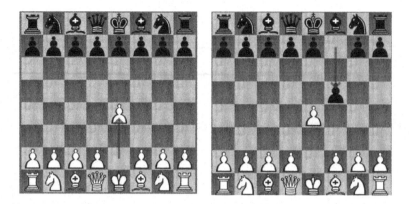

2. exf5...g6

3. Be2...g6xf5

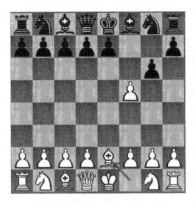 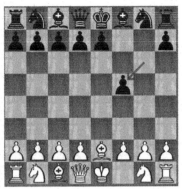

4. Bh5++. White checkmates Black on the 4th move. Black cannot move the King, take the attacker or block the check with another piece.

The Middle Game

Here are some important Middle Game Principles:

- ✓ Develop your pieces, minor pieces first.

- ✓ Castle at some point. Protect your King.

- ✓ Look for weaknesses: unguarded players; Pawns at rear end of a chain.

- ✓ Take (capture) toward the center with your Pawns. It controls more squares.

- ✓ Move your Rooks to open or half open files. Think about doubling them up on the same file. This is powerful. An *open file* is a column where there are no players in front of your Rook. A *half open file* is a column on which there is only one of your enemy's Pawns.

- ✓ Block your opponents' attacks. Don't give them any breathing room.

- ✓ Think of a plan. Plans can be simple or complicated. One or two moves ahead, or more than that. Use "What if?" or "How do I?" thinking.

- ✓ Try to create combinations and employ creative attacks.

✓ Don't immediately recoil from attacks. Counterattack to give your opponent tough choices: Take this and lose that? Trade?

✓ Exchange pieces if you have more Pawns than your opponent. You want to end up with nothing but Pawns and the King, with you having the most Pawns on the board.

✓ Master Basic Checkmates: You goal is to win here and not go to an Endgame. For this to happen you need to know some basic checkmates. We are going to briefly review three: two Rooks, one Rook and the King, and the Queen and the King. I would highly recommend going online to review these and more.

Before we get into that, we are going to review some special attacks.

Special Attacks

There are six special attacks and strategies with which you should become thoroughly familiar:

1. The Fork: Attacking two or more pieces at once.

2. The Pin: Attacking a less valuable piece in front of a more valuable piece on the same file, rank or diagonal.

51

3. The Skewer or X-Ray: Attacking a more valuable piece in front of a less valuable piece on the same file, rank, or diagonal.

4. The Discovered Attack: Moving one of your players out of the way to reveal an attack or check.

5. The Double and Triple Team Attack: Two or three or more pieces teaming up for a coordinated attack. Always try to use as many pieces as possible to coordinate your attack. Since most beginners and casual players try to win with major pieces, winning with minor pieces can be most rewarding. It can be used in defense too: two or three pieces could be protecting the square.

6. The Sacrifice: Intentionally getting captured to gain advantage.

Using these attacks and strategies is fun and rewarding. We will demonstrate each, one by one.

The Fork

Forks can be simple. On the board on the right, it was black's move and he pushed[6] his Pawn to f6, forking two white Knights.

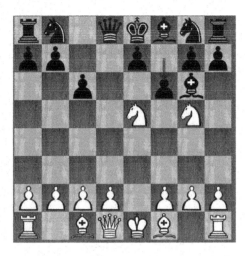

On this board, Black attacked the White Knight with his Pawn on f6 so the Knight moved to Ne6. In doing so he forked the Black Queen and the Bishop.

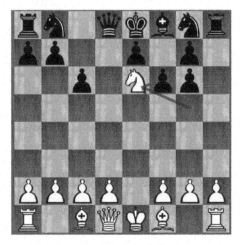

---

[6] "pushing" a Pawn means moving the Pawn forward.

The Black Queen responds by attacking the White Knight, but neglects to see the fantastic opening for White: a Knight triple fork!

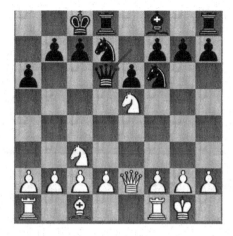

Nf7! attacking the Black Queen and both Rooks. Black resigned at this point.

The Pin

The pin is when a less valuable player is attacked on the same line as a more valuable player, rendering the attacked piece frozen and unable to move.

In this example, oblivious of the danger, the White Queen has moved to c3: Qc3... Note the Black Rook on the half open b file. It has most of the file protected. Note the  Black Bishop on d6 which then moves to c4.

... Bb4!! And the Queen is pinned! If the White Queen takes the Black Bishop, she gets taken by the Black Rook.

The Skewer

A *Skewer* is the opposite of a pin. A more valuable player is attacked in the same line as a less valuable player, so it is compelled to move or be captured.

In this example the White King must move because it is in check. The result is the capture of the White Queen. A perfect skewer!

The Discovered Attack

Pictured here, the Black Queen has moved from e4 to f4 to avoid being capture.
But that opened up a huge opportunity for white. What Black didn't see was a devastating discovered attack.

Bc6+! (Bishop to c6, check!) Since the Black King must now get out of check by moving or taking the White Bishop, the Black Queen is a goner on White's next move: Rook takes Queen! Rxf4!

57

The Triple Team

In this final move of a 20-move game, three minor pieces cause checkmate. The last move is Nf7++, and the King has nowhere to go. As you progress, see if you can win with minor pieces.

The Sacrifice

The Sacrifice is letting a player be captured for the aim of completing a secret plan, like checkmate. It can be offered as a lure or it can be a non-choice. I offer here one example of calculated sacrifice by the man who literally wrote the book on sacrifice, Rudoph Spielmann[7]. This is one of the most famous Queen Sacrifice games in chess history. Rudolph Spielman (White) vs. Baldur Hoelinger (Black), Vienna, 1929.

---

[7] Rudolph Spielmann literally wrote the book: "The Art of Sacrifice in Chess," originally published simultaneously in German and English in 1935.

This game might look a little complicated but we are at the very end and it is worth sticking with it.

We pick up with move 25 in a 28-move game. Take a good look at the entire board, in particular, Spielman's Bishops, aimed directly at the "King's corner," and note his White Queen on h6. The white Knight had just made a brilliant move to e7+.

25. Ne7+...

...Qxe7, sacrificing the Knight and drawing the Black Queen to e7.

Here comes the
next sacrifice:

26. Qh7+ ...

(White Queen
to h7 and check!)

...Kxh7, and the
Black King takes
the White
Queen. (It's his
only move.) Note
the position of
the White
Bishops: Dark
Square Bishop
covering the

entire dark diagonal, and the Light Square Bishop pinning
the g6 black Pawn..

27. Rh5+ ...

(Rook to h5 check!)

...Kg8 Since the g6 Pawn is pinned, g8 is the King's only move to escape check; and note the position of the Dark Square, White Bishop. The Black Queen is powerless being lured away by the Knight sacrifice.

28. Rh8++ Rook to h8 and checkmate!

Basic Checkmates

1. The "Rook Roller," is also called Ladder's Mate. The idea is to push the King to one side of the board for the final trap by alternating Rooks. In this example, we start with this board and it's white's move:

Kh6...

...Raa3 (Rook on the a file to a3) and the King is forced down to g5 or h5.

62

This is how it looks when all the moves are put on one board.

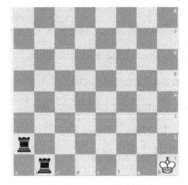

With this as the final position:

King and One Rook Mate.

In this example the black Rook and King are the attackers. The idea is to force your opponent's King to a back or side rank using the Rook as a "force field," and King "opposition." The "force field" is the rank on which the King cannot stay because he would be in check, and the "opposition" are the three squares in front of your King to which white cannot move.

The idea is to push the King to the back rank directly in front of the black King, then move the black Rook and check the King on the back rank. Checkmate because the Kings are on the same file and the three squares in front of the white King are blocked, while being in check from the Rook. Go online to any chess site to see the details.

Queen and King Mate

There are so many variations of this mate, that I'm just going to give you marching orders: Limit the opposing King's movement with your Queen, then move the King closer and closer.

A word of caution: it is easy to inadvertently create a draw by not giving the opposing King choices. Be careful in your eagerness to win so that you don't create a situation where the opposing King is not in check but cannot move.

I would highly recommend going online to see these and more checkmates explained in a more dynamic fashion.

The Endgame

There is no exact definition of when the Endgame begins, but most chess players would say that the Endgame has begun when there is an abundance of Pawns on the board and there is a scarcity of pieces. In this book, we are going to assume that the endgame is when only Pawns and the King are on the board.

As you are playing and learning, you have reached the endgame when you realize that your King might be able to attack and capture something, because there aren't any major pieces left to attack him, and you would be correct. In the endgame, the King does become an attacker.

This also means that you will need to master the "Pawn Game." The game is great practice and simple. You begin the game with only Pawns. The objective and the win is to be the first one to get a Pawn promoted. The Pawn Game is great because you can practice blocking and en passant. Go online see more of this. I have my students play Pawn games before every session. Kids love to play this game with a fast clock too, like one minute per side.

The Endgame has its own set of principles, and here are some.

65

1. In the Endgame, your King is powerful. Realize that and use him as an attacker.

2. Centralize your King and begin attacking and supporting him.

3. Take advantage of three on two, or two on one Pawn situations. Draw your opponent into allowing you a passed Pawn. A passed Pawn is one that is "behind enemy lines." That is, your opponent's chance to get him before promotion looks futile.

4. "In the endgame, the King is Queen!"[8]

5. In the endgame, slow down! Many foolish mistakes are made by moving too quickly.

6. Get your King involved.

7. Don't ignore Pawns on the flank.

8. Wipe out enemy Pawns in your territory during the Middle Game. If you don't, in the Endgame they will become like land mines: exploding when you least expect them too.

---

[8] *The author, playing with a friend, after a few tequila shooters.*

What follows is a list of principles to incorporate into your game. Some overlap what I've just told you, and some don't. Keep them handy as you improve.

52 Chess Principles In No Particular Order

1. Open with a center Pawn.
2. Develop Knights before Bishops.
3. Try to develop your Knights towards the center. Remember, "Knights on the rim are grim."
4. Don't cramp or block your pieces.
5. Trapped Bishops are useless.
6. When pieces are blocked, free them.
7. Control the center.
8. Don't move the same piece twice in a row.
9. Always ask yourself, "Can he put me in check or win a piece?"
10. Every move should have a purpose.
11. Ask yourself, "Why did he move there?" after each opponent move.
12. If you have more pieces on the board than your opponent, you are "up the exchange." When you are up the exchange, trade pieces, not Pawns.
13. Never leave pieces unprotected.
14. If you are losing, don't give up fighting. Look for counterplay.

15. If you are in doubt of an opponent's sacrifice, accept it.

16. Attack with as many Pawns and pieces as possible.

17. Exchange pieces if it helps your development.

18. Don't bring your Queen out early.

19. Castle strategically, neither too soon nor too late, or not at all.

20. Develop Rooks to open files.

21. Put Rooks behind passed Pawns.

22. Keep your King as far away from the center as possible, except in the endgame.

23. In the endgame, use your King for offense.

24. Don't castle if it brings your King into greater danger from attack.

25. After castling, don't break the Pawn formation around your King.

26. Attack on the opposite color of your opponent's lone Bishop.

27. Counter attack in the center when your opponent is attacking your flank.

28. If your Bishops are blocked, trade pieces.

29. In crowded centers, Knights trump Bishops.

30. In open centers, Bishops trump Knights.

31. Keep your opponent cramped.

32. Look for tactics and combinations/Create tactics and combinations.

33. Double Rooks, or double a Rook and the Queen, on open files.

34. After deciding on your move, always ask yourself "Can I make a better one?"

35. When deciding on your next move, not considering your opponent's threats is suicide.

36. See the whole board before every move.

37. Watch your time and avoid time trouble.

38. A Knight works better with a Bishop than another Knight.

39. Connect your Rooks on your back rank.

40. Protect advancing Pawns with Rooks on the same file.

41. Move your Rooks to an open file.

42. When capturing with Pawns, capture toward the center.

43. Try to avoid doubled Pawns.

44. Try to avoid isolated Pawns. (Pawns with no Pawns on adjacent files.)

45. Try to avoid backward Pawns. (Backward Pawns are when adjacent Pawns have moved ahead.)

46. Attack the back Pawn in a Pawn chain.

47. Don't trade a Bishop for a Knight.

48. White Rooks on the 7th rank are strong.

49. Black Rooks on the 2nd rank are strong.

50. Use Knights to block imminent Pawn promotion.

51. Everyone blunders. Get over it.

52. Know when to ignore these principles!

I encourage you to experiment and just play the game. Play with your kid. They love it. Play often. If any part of the book leaves you with a question, immediately research it. Play online. Chess.com or other sites do this automatically. Just sign up for free, create a user name[9], and start playing.

In Part II of this book we will explore the reach and power of chess. We will see how it has touched many parts of our human existence.

---

[9] Mine is "Edward_Book"

PART II: Why Chess Matters

Chess as a metaphor for war has been expanded and it is now understood to apply to much more than its military-oriented origins. In addition to being great fun to play, it has been transformed from a pastime for kings and intellectuals into an educational tool for all. Therefore, its advantages extend far beyond mastering an antiquated game on a checkerboard of 64 bright and dark squares that has peculiar pieces, a quirky "language," and is played by an elite few.

The game influences a wide variety of human endeavors including history, art and design, psychology, sociology and the business world.

Introduced into your family, it can be a long lasting and cherished quality of your shared experiences, but it is more than that. It is especially beneficial to parents and teachers because it gives them access to an important but neglected aspect of educating kids, namely the learned attitudes and behaviors necessary for success and happiness.

Currently, chess is included in a thorough list of activities outside the typical educational curriculum. A quick online search reveals chess is one of many extracurricular activities offered by most schools. I highly recommend all students participate in as many extracurricular activities that parents and kids can handle. They help develop talents, interests

71

and passions, and many can teach practical skills. They also help broaden students' knowledge and experience and are rated very highly by college administrators when evaluating student candidates for admission, not to mention future bosses during job interviews.

Why single out chess? Chess is uniquely beneficial as it provides young people a foundation for critical thinking, bold moves, and self-confidence. With chess being part of a child's extracurricular activities, *all* interests and activities, in school and out, become richer due to the skills and mindset chess brings to the individual.

We begin by examining the aesthetic side of chess in Chapter 4. Chess has made an enormous contribution to our language, art and history. We will see just a few examples.

In Chapter 5 we explore chess and psychology with an emphasis on development and learning, through the lens of the relatively new field of Positive Psychology.

In Chapter 6, we take the framework learned in the previous chapter and apply it to school, home and family.

In Chapter 7, we delve into how a career can benefit from chess.

Chapter 8 is about Chess and Junior Golf Programs.

With this in mind, I invite you to explore the ideas presented in the rest of this book.

Chapter Four: Art, History & Other Tidbits

Discoveries in archeology amaze us as we find the precursors of chess to be over 2000 years old. Ancient chessboards, murals, and mosaics dot historical sites worldwide.

Spain was a learning center in Moorish times. Here is a parchment from "Libro de Juegos," (the book of games).

Ancient Chess Set, circa 800 AD

Circa 1283. It shows a chess problem.

Chess has been the subject of many famous pieces of art. The oil painting by Ludwig Deutch imagines two Merchant Moors playing chess.

*Ludwig Deutch –
the Chess Game, 1896*

Ben Franklin was an avid chess player and wrote one of the

first expositions on chess in the newly formed United States written in Columbia Magazine. "The Morals of Chess," was published in 1786 and explained how to play the game and the lessons learned from it.

Ben Franklin with Lord & Lady Howe

When traveling abroad, Franklin arranged a secret meeting with Lord Howe under the guise of playing chess with his wife.

The famous American painter Thomas Eakins used a chess game to depict some complex relationships in his life.

Eakins - The Chess Players, 1876

Although it appears to be just two players and an observer, the work, like chess itself, is a metaphor for Eakin's relationships with the participants in the painting. The observer is his father, and the older gentleman on the left is a professor of French Literature. On the right is a younger man who is an artist. Both players were former teachers of Eakin's. Notice that his father is not in the game and the younger player is winning with his queen still on the board. According to some art historians, this depicts Eakin's distant relationship with his father, and with the younger man winning, this shows his desire to overcome his father's dominance. If you are a Dad and you have a son that wants to play chess with you, this painting will become very meaningful. There is nothing a young son wants more than to experience his first win over his Dad. It's a primal thing.

Current media is also filled with chess references. The latest and most popular book turned tv series, "The Queen's Gambit," was a huge success in literally every civilized country. Little Chess Queens are popping up all over the world!

Harry Potter has made chess even more popular.

Cartoon characters have made their way to the chessboard.

The Simpsons Chess Game

Interior design, furniture, and even chess piece design and themes, have all contributed to the depth and breadth of this ancient game.

A chess set, table and chairs adds class to any interior.

Chess has been infused into our language too.

- Who wants to be a "Pawn" in the game of life?

- Or a Pawn in company politics?

- Who hasn't said, "What's my next move?"

This came from chess.

Other Tidbits[10]

➢ Chess Master in Britain were used as code breakers in WWII.

➢ The Spanish innovation of allowing pawns to advance two squares on their first move instead of one was introduced in 1280.

➢ The Soviet Union held the Soyez-9 crew's first chess game on June 9, 1970. The game took place between space and Earth, with both sides having an equal number of pieces. The game ended in a draw.

---

[10] These interesting facts came from chess.com and the thechessjournal.com

- The name "Checkmate" comes from the Persian term "Shah Mat," which means "the King is slain."

- A chess book was the second book published in English. It was translated and printed from French into English by William Caxton in 1474.

- Chess is a popular game that has been shown to improve memory function—often mentioned in psychology books as a highly effective way to advance one's intelligence. It also allows the player's mind to work through a variety of complicated issues while solving them.

- Chess is highly beneficial against Alzheimer's disease.

- Chess has been clinically tested and shown to drastically improve kids' grades and other mental and cognitive functions.

- On the TV show Star Trek, Kirk and Spock have engaged in three chess games. All three games were won by Kirk.

- The world's most expensive chess set, the magnificent Jewel Royale Chess Set, commissioned by the Royale Jewel Company and created in Great Britain, includes diamonds and emeralds, is worth than $9.8 million.

➢ The oldest chess manual known to have existed was written in Arabic and originated around 840.

The previous pages were a small glimpse of what is out there. I would encourage you to explore more online.

Chapter Five: Chess & Psychology

Around 1996, a psychologist named Martin Seligman had a revelation. He happened to be president of the American Psychological Association at the time looking after the entire field. With that bird's eye view, he began to think the field was missing something by just focusing on eliminating misery. Getting rid of illnesses like alcoholism, addiction, depression, schizophrenia and a host of other maladies is a good thing isn't it? Well, yes and no. Just because you eliminate disease, doesn't mean you will be happy and successful.

He started asking questions. Why not be curious about success, happiness and well-being? Why are successful people successful? How do couples get and stay happily married for years and years? He came to this conclusion: he suggested that the field not abandon the noble cause of eliminating misery but add a new focus: *Start exploring what makes life worth living and the conditions surrounding it.* Focus on wellness and well-being and how to achieve it. With these and other inquiries, the new field of Positive Psychology was born.

Foundations of Positive Psychology

We have learned a lot since Dr. Seligman created Positive Psychology. We now know we can learn and create the conditions within ourselves and our environment to live our best life possible, filled with happiness, well-being and contentment. Two basic tenants[11] of well-being are *accomplishment* and *engagement* and they are closely related.

Accomplishment, in light of Positive Psychology, is not only completing a final task or reaching a final goal. It is that, but just as important are the experiences both positive and negative that got you to your goal.[12] A typical description of these experiences are *success* or *failure,* but this framework for a young person comes with a price, as they assume this is who they are, at least for the moment. Over time successive failures may convince one that he is a failure. But successive positive achievements can be dangerous too. Both situations are precarious. One leads to self-hate and depression and the other leads to the *impostor syndrome.* "I'm a phony. I'm not really this good. What if I get found out?"

These interim experiences may be re-framed three ways, either as sub-goals, process goals or a "system." Some of them move you toward your final objective and some don't, and they are neither good nor bad. From this vantage point,

---

[11] There are more.

[12] If you haven't reached your goal, then you aren't finished!

people shift away from success or failure and instead turn these interim events into *lessons*.

This is particularly important for kids because they are often too sensitive about learning. They don't understand that what is called, "failure," is really an intense learning experience. They take failure personally. They wrap up their self-worth in the moment and can be devastated if they make a mistake or get out-witted during a game. By re-framing the mindset of "winning and losing" to "winning and learning," it takes *you* out of the identity of success or failure. *You* are neither a success nor a failure. Success and failure are both temporary conditions. They are not you. This feeling, this realization, is very reassuring to kids. It bolsters their self-image and improves self-confidence. When reinforced by parents or teachers, a rock solid confidence appears.

Another thing happens when you reframe success and failure into a learning experience. You can revisit reaching, or not reaching, your sub-goals as successes or failures if you want to, but it doesn't affect you as they did before. You can take and leave what you will from the experiences, and you are still the person who is happy, striving and accepted.

Chess is winning and learning to the max. In chess, some moves work and others don't; it's just part of the game.

85

What looks like a hopeless situation changes in an instant when a move suddenly "appears" in your mind's eye. If you play chess, you know what I mean. A feeling hits you like you've found gold in the desert. Worry changes to hope and confidence.

When viewed through this lens, chess becomes a microcosm of purposeful action. As a parent, you can use the analogy of a chess game for just about any life segment that involves goals or self-improvement. You might say that chess is mind training for goal-seekers.

Another benefit of chess is it promotes focus on overcoming obstacles. After all, the whole game might be defined as overcoming multiple, successive obstacles. As kids get into chess, since this is just part of the game, they get accustomed to handling obstacles. Problems are transformed into situations that can be handled or solved. What happens here is what Piaget would call, "accommodation," new information that transforms your worldview or self-image. It doesn't happen all at once, but overtime, the young player develops an underlying mindset of confidence and this in turn promotes optimism.

We are still left with one question. How should we experience the experiences? For insight here, we turn to *engagement.*

Engagement for the purpose of positive psychology doesn't mean just doing something. It means to lose yourself in your task at hand. Time and space disappear. You and your task are one. The optimum condition of this state is called, "Flow."

There is an additional observation and that is the quality called "grit," a term popularized by Angela Duckworth. Grit might be defined as perseverance driven by passion. Grit also demonstrates conscientiousness, which means one has reliability, is trustworthy, and keeps true to one's word.

Mindsets

The ideas discussed so far fit right into a concept called "Mindset." This concept was beautifully presented in the book by Carol. S. Dweck, Ph.D., "Mindset, the New Psychology of Success." She demonstrates in great detail two mindsets and the effects each have on every part of living. They are the *Growth Mindset* and the *Fixed Mindset.*

The *growth mindset* is a belief that you are firmly in control of your destiny. *You* can change, grow, learn and succeed in spite of birth conditions both personal and environmental. In this mindset, purposeful practice, training and perseverance are its hallmarks. There is no room for self-blame, blaming others, blaming circumstances, blaming traits, heredity, culture or tradition. Talent, God-given abilities and tendencies, although much appreciated, are secondary to hard work. There now have been many studies demonstrating that people with a growth mindset are much more successful than most. The opposite of the growth mindset is *the fixed mindset.*

The *fixed mindset* is a *belief* that turns the growth mindset upside down. It is the belief that you are not in control and not much will help, including effort. The fixed mindset is rigid. It is why people remain unhappy in careers to relationships yet do nothing about it. Educational research has discovered that the fixed mindset is a path to mediocrity and unhappiness.

We tend to be a blend of both mindsets and we do have choices. To illustrate the point, I offer the following: There is a Cherokee parable that frames this choice beautifully. A grandfather is teaching his grandson about life. "A fight is going on inside me," he said to the boy. "It is a terrible fight and it is between two wolves. One is *evil: he is anger, envy, entitlement, self-pity, resentment, hopelessness, and inferiority.*" He continued, "The other is good: he is *hope, optimism, self-confidence, enthusiasm, kindness, and industry.* The same fight is going on inside you my grandson – and inside every other person, too." The grandson thought about it for a minute and then asked his grandfather, "Which wolf will win?" The grandfather replied simply, "The one you feed."

Our goal as humans is to feed the growth mindset and starve the fixed mindset.

To review, *accomplishment* and *engagement* are key factors in improving your life journey. The *fixed mindset* is the road to frustration and unhappiness. Having a growth *mindset* is the catalyst for success and happiness.

Understanding and living the growth mindset are key in establishing the qualities of optimism, curiosity, self-confidence, and an improved self-image.

Remember, we are tying chess to all this, and you will soon see how it fits into the growth mindset.

As a parent or educator, what do you do about it? How do parents or teachers take an active role? This brings us to the next chapter.

Chapter Six: Kid Stuff

One of the ways kids learn about the world is through play. As adults, why do we forget this idea? We tend to trivialize play, especially kids' play. After all, we are grownups dealing with somber stuff. We have responsibilities like a serious education, a family and a career. We believe play is a pastime where we can forget all pressure and relax. Play is a way to get the kids out of our hair, and the principle of *kids learning through play* is not in our thinking. I'm suggesting the idea of *kids learning through play* should be taken just as seriously as the learning which occurs in school, or anywhere else for that matter.

Perhaps you are now thinking if play is so important, is there a game that could provide kids with really important life habits and guidelines that could help them succeed throughout their lives?

The Game of Life

I humbly suggest that chess is that game. While being enormously fun to play, the underlying skills employed are the same skills employed when living a successful life. Chess creates competitive learning experiences and kids love playing it, especially with their parents.

Let's talk about learning, beginning with how *fun* fits in. Fun is the pleasurable feeling one gets when enthusiasm seems to appear out of nowhere. This creates sustained

91

interest coupled with curiosity and awe. To me, fun and learning are twins. They crowd out winning and losing. When I'm playing chess, even when I lose, I'm having fun, especially when I lose to a combination that was right in front of me and I didn't see it. I do not feel sorry for myself; I'm glad for my competitor. Of course, if a combination appears before me, I'm delighted, but critically, I'm amazed and appreciative of what chess just presented to the both of us. It didn't matter what brain it came from. This is an example of what? You guessed it. The *growth mindset!* Although I lost the game, I didn't lose, I learned. Do I still want to win? Of course. Am I a loser? Of course not!

How Most Adults See Things

Most adults have fairly simple views when it comes to school and play. School is where you learn and play is where you unwind from the pressures of school, just like adults do with work. After all, work is where the pressure is on, a place where you are forced to be in order to eat and pay rent. Adult recreational play is the escape from that. Play is a place to unwind, relax and forget about deadlines, your lousy boss and your irritating co-workers. Validating our belief about the role of school and play, sure enough at 3pm, we see kids run around like maniacs, letting off steam, escaping the pressures of school.

Another adult belief is we think school is an information factory, and the key activity is remembering facts and regurgitating them on a test. Twelve years of cramming information into a kids' head makes them ready to enter the world of work, and after a period of adjustment, take their rightful place. Ordinary adults don't give much thought to the underlying skills that are needed in addition to the information learned in school. The more the "factory" has crammed in, the more that a kid can regurgitate, which supposedly equals success in life. So school is where you learn traditional subjects. English, math, history, health, science, social studies, government, gym class, etc. Well, something has happened recently that has affected all that.

Like Dr. Seligman's insight regarding the field of psychology, parents and educators have discovered a whole new realm in education. One that has been hidden for most of the modern era of schooling and it is composed of several components and referred to as "non-cognitive skills."

Throughout the early 1990s and for the following several years, many children were showing up to kindergarten "not prepared," according to some kindergarten teachers. Research showed that better educated, and more successful parents had more books in the house and spoke more words in the life of a three year old, than less educated and less successful parents.

Scholars jumped to the conclusion that more words and information was the answer, and an industry was born that tried to cram words and ideas into the heads of kids from birth to kindergarten. Remember Baby Einstein and Baby Mozart?

After a few years and for a variety of reasons, scholars started to question the notion that cramming words and ideas into a kid's brain from birth to five years old wasn't necessarily the answer. They started to look all over the spectrum of education, from pre-school to college, and started asking questions. Who got good grades and who didn't? Who succeeded in college and who didn't? Who was most successful after college and who wasn't?

Essential Skills

Focusing on success in college, they found what really matters is a set of skills which had been overlooked. They are (1) knowing how to *study effectively and proficiently* (2) having the necessary *work habits* ingrained into your behavior (3) using time to your advantage with good *time management* (4) employing *help-seeking behavior,* (5) understanding *social problem solving* and (6) knowing how to *solve academic problems.*

More questions arose. When do you teach these and how? Is it possible to teach them effectively or teach them at all? Are they mostly part of a child's genetic makeup and hard to teach or improve upon? (Are fixed and growth mindsets coming to mind?)

Many of these behaviors have traditionally been in the domain of the culture, clan, or family, and not looked at with a critical eye. It was part of your makeup when you arrived in school. It was just who you were and where you came from; it's just what you learn naturally as you grow up. The "factory" threw information at you for you to ingest. Time management and the rest of that stuff was the kid's problem and off the educational system's radar.

Essential Qualities

Well along came other research that uncovered even more qualities necessary for success. These qualities are *curiosity, gratitude, conscientiousness, grit, optimism, self-control and social intelligence.* How interesting! Educators had discovered the foundation for teaching the *Growth Mindset!*

The field of Positive Psychology has studied and emphasized these qualities for the past 25 years. We have universal agreement that these qualities need to be taught to children starting at an early age, and it turns out that chess is one way to do that. *Chess, when taught and learned the right way, is Growth Mindset Training. It is Positive Psychology in action.*

95

Are you thinking incredulously, "So I should give my kid curiosity lessons?" The answer is, "Yes," and it is better to start sooner rather than later. Ideally, around five years old. What about those other qualities? Yes, those too. Since this is a book about chess, you might be thinking the obvious, that I think that chess is the answer to world peace but allow me to explain.

When I say chess is the answer, and you are thinking, "Soccer!" you are almost there. Go to the end note for more information![i] But seriously, there are a lot of things (games and experiences) that are beneficial to the growth of a child. Like Martin Seligman suggested to the entire field of psychology to expand its horizons to include Positive Psychology, I am suggesting that you think out of the box with chess. In fact, if you remember in the first section of Part II, I recommended extracurricular activities. I would encourage a multi-dimensional approach to a kid's learning experience with participation in a team sport, an individual sport or skill, drawing, a musical instrument, and chess.

So how does chess "teach" Curiosity, Gratitude, Grit, Optimism, Self-Control and Social Intelligence and therefore promote the growth mindset? Well, it doesn't by itself, but with a well-informed instructor, these qualities can be explained, discussed and understood by your children or students.

It is important to teach anything correctly and chess is no exception. You wouldn't throw a kid in a room with a violin and some sheet music and say, "See you in six months at your first recital! And keep it down, I'm busy!"

Growth Mindset Lessons

What follows are ideas and suggestions on how to use chess to teach the qualities we've been exploring. Using the framework of scope and reach gives you a base from which to explore.

One thing to keep in mind is even though you are the parent or the teacher, you are learning together with your child or student. Even though you may know chess and the qualities you are teaching, you are also learning about your student, even if that student is your own child. They are growing and changing in mind and body right before your eyes. Participate in the changes and you too will enjoy and experience his or her enthusiasm, and your enthusiasm is great for kids. As you experience the joy in your child or student's learning, that joy becomes contagious, and joy is the foundation for enthusiasm. These qualities put your kids into the frame of mind from which they can do their very best, which is the essence of the growth mindset.

Getting specific, here are some point-by-point suggestions.

Curiosity

Kids are naturally curious. When you enthusiastically tell them startling facts, like the scope of chess, they want more. For example, there are more chess moves than grains of sand on every beach on earth! Or there are more moves in chess than there are stars in the milky way! Research facts online together! Your kid will love it. These are examples of scope.

Next go to examples of reach. Go to famous historic games, famous people that played chess like Ben Franklin. Then go to current people, actors, athletes, etc.

Ben Franklin played chess and wrote the first essay on chess in America. Abraham Lincoln played chess. Teddy Roosevelt played chess. Movie stars play chess: Julia Roberts, Nicolas Cage, are examples. Sports stars play chess: Joe Burrow, the Superbowl QB of the Cincinnati Bengals, Kobe Bryant (basketball), Bobby Jones (golf). Singers: Frank Sinatra, Madonna, John Lennon. Even Princess Diana played chess.

Go online together, read books together, discover together and get enthused together. Kids will love the teamwork type search, with the team being you and him or her. Let them do the "clicking," and you help if needed. Point out different things; respond to your kid's observations. You will experience excitement without judgement. You will set up the foundation for future conversations, and not just about chess either. You might ignite curiosity from super novae to a beach on some remote land, to why Ben Franklin dressed the way he did.

Kids respond to how big things are and how famous people act, and you are the most famous person they know, and playing chess with the most famous person they know is extremely rewarding to them.

Optimism

Kids are naturally optimistic too. As your child or student gets awed by the scope of chess, learns how to play, has fun playing, wins and learns, it fosters optimism. More fun is to come. That means more learning and more "Aha!" moments together. Rejoice in those.

Conscientiousness

Conscientiousness is demonstrated primarily by showing responsibility and reliability. This means sticking with something no matter what obstacles

99

appear, and staying with it to the end, not giving up or giving up hope; not letting people down, including yourself. You should support and encourage this.

Conscientiousness gets easier because of optimism. There are always exciting new worlds to discover and new adventures to be had.

The concept of planning helps too. Adults should encourage planning and not just making random moves. "Your opponent's Queen is out to early. What's your plan to capture it?" for example.

Grit

Grit is similar to conscientiousness but on a gut level. Grit is the power to persevere. Grit is more about inner power and self-confidence. Playing chess with adult encouragement and support teaches grit. Grit is sticking to it because you are "learning, not losing."

Self-control

Moving too quickly is a common mistake in chess. (And in life for that matter!). Teaching kids to not move too soon is huge. Beginners and especially children, tend to be impulsive. Teaching kids to identify when they are being impulsive and then explaining how to create choices teaches patience, which is a hallmark of self-control. Employing self-control can take you a long way not only in chess but in life.

Self-confidence

As kids play and learn how to play better, their self-confidence grows. Mistakes aren't the end of the world and they don't mean you are failure. An encouraging word from a parent or teacher reinforces self-confidence. No one is a *born winner* or a *born loser.* We are all people who are playing the game of life and some moves are better than others.

Social Intelligence

Social intelligence is how you handle interaction with other people. How to compete without being abrasive is one key factor. I have all my students start a game with a handshake and wish their opponent, "Good Luck!" At the end of each game, we shake hands again and say, "Good Game!" One can feel great about winning, but being empathetic to the loser is taking the high road. In my observations over the years, these two behaviors are always accompanied with a smile. Oh, and it used to be called, "good manners!"

How to be a Growth Minded Parent

There is only one way. Demonstrate your love of learning by researching and learning with your kids. Be enthusiastic, and they will see it, feel it, and love it. You can still be a parent and share observations and thoughts with your kid. You'll be the best teacher they ever had.

As a parent you now need to change your focus away from results, and I don't mean that you should ignore them. Your focus should be two things: the *effort put in* and *the experience of that effort*. Did you apply yourself correctly? Were there distractions? Correct acknowledgement of winning and losing is important. Do not minimize "failures," or overreact to successes. Each is a product of effort plus circumstance. Your job as a parent is to help the child analyze and evaluate why it happened without judgment. And this is key as you can be very happy about success, and very sad about failure, *but internalize the effort not the event.* Remember, as great as a win is, and as hurtful as a loss is, in the big picture, in the growth mindset, they are simply both learning events.

Timing

It's never too late but the earlier the better. I don't mean teaching the king's gambit at crib side, but depending on the child's curiosity, (of which you now should be a part), age 5 or 6 is not too early, but don't force it. You might even

102

see signs earlier, which will make you feel great, but you may also see signs later, but this should not make you feel bad. It's just life. Einstein flunked math in elementary school.

By the time a kid is a teenager, it might be hard to pin him or her down but look for moments. Perhaps before bedtime, but not too late, or maybe a weekend morning might be a good time to play. With a teen, you want to create comfort, and with whom you ultimately want to have adult conversations. Your goal should be to have them include you in their decision making process by valuing your feedback.

Summary

Chess creates a safe space that introduces similar feelings when facing real-world consequences, but without any life-altering results. It effectively becomes a low-stakes training environment. It can encourage kids to overcome the fear of leaving their comfort zone and experience the related benefits as a result. This makes chess an excellent tool for personal growth.

Personal growth is demonstrated in the following chart of chess learning taxonomy. Just like a budding playwright or novelist goes through stages of learning, the same is true for chess players. What is less evident are the skills developed since they are "non-cognitive." A skilled parent can see them, and with your newfound knowledge discovered in this book, as an enlightened parent you will be able to see and develop these skills in your children!

Chapter Seven: Your Career and Chess

It is interesting how an ancient game created as a metaphor for war, has been transformed into an educational tool for kids. But it goes beyond that. There are observations and lessons that provide additional perspectives regarding your career.

For the purpose of looking at your career using chess, let's call it the chess mindset. It might seem simplistic, but maybe that is what you need to sometimes evaluate and analyze things from a different point of view.

Your career involves moves and responses just like in a chess game. When you get up in the morning and select the clothes you will wear that day, that is a move and the world responds. When your boss fires you or you are laid off unexpectedly, it's your move. You analyze conditions on the board. That is, you evaluate your career situation now that this event has occurred. You do some planning, make moves and get responses. You get hired! You are the Pawn that got promoted! And so it goes. You make a move, deal with the responses, then move again, repeat, move again and the game of life and career is on.

Your career involves a lot of people and chess gives you a team of people of varying talents on your side. You can employ them in combinations as you wish. That is, they are battling with you and an enemy is trying to destroy you.

105

From your chess training you now know that learning can be both painful and fun, but nevertheless, all experiences are valuable. Winning isn't everything but winning is better than losing, even though you now know how to keep your wits about you when you lose. You have learned that if you don't plan, even just a little bit, your outcomes are totally out of your control. You have learned that if you make a mistake, you can overcome it. You are self-confident that you can because you've done it before.

Is that all there is? Well, yes and no. I have come to these conclusions about career[13]. One, competition exists. Two, there are no solutions, only trade-offs. Three, you aren't your results. Four, there are limiting beliefs that do not have to exist. Five, there is a power, greater than you and all of humanity. We will now explore these ideas.

Competition

The big mistake people make is to ignore competition. They actually don't see it, and pretend that it doesn't exist, minimize it or trivialize it, because they don't know how to handle it. Or they become fearful and anxious because they've never practiced handling competition in a difficult setting.

---

[13] And life perhaps?

Competing is scary, it's hard work, and can destroy your ego, self-esteem, happiness, bring on fear, make you depressed. It can also make you feel anger when you lose. You may be angry at your opponent, angry at yourself, angry at your parents, teachers and coaches for not giving you the right coaching or guidance.

The reality is not everyone understands that they are experiencing competition when it is happening to them. Not everyone is athletic or skilled at something and has had experience competing, winning and losing. Some people just choose not to participate. Well, as I said at the beginning of this chapter, it's there whether you choose to believe it or not.

How does chess help? It gives you the mind map of an experienced competitor. You can think like a savvy business person with the inner calm of a zen master. Life is competitive just like chess is competitive. You have time to think and make a move and see what happens. (99% of the time anyway!) Chess also provides *character training (remember grit?)* which is required to persevere in the face of stiff competition.

Trade-Offs

The second mistake people make is to view the world as if there are only problems and solutions, when in real life there are mostly *problems and tradeoffs,* with solutions being exceedingly rare.

Remember the fork in chess? When your Queen and a Knight are being attacked, that tradeoff is easy: save your Queen. It almost feels like a "solution." But in reality, most of your decisions in life is like being forked on the chess board with your Knight and Bishop being attacked. The pieces have the same value so there are other factors to consider. There is no "solution" to the situation you are in. Your only move is a tradeoff, just like life.

Tradeoffs, whether perceived or not, are choices, and choices are decisions. And as we all know, decisions have consequences. Consequences are multi-dimensional. Their effects can be long or short-term, and intended or unintended. But they also have reach and scope. Reach means how long, that is, *duration*, and scope means how *widespread.* It is best to be aware of this.

The third mistake people make is to tie their self-worth to results: winning or losing; having or not having. Happier people do not do this exclusively. There are many rich, unhappy workaholics and we look at them and think, "What a waste! All that time and effort, all those toys, and they never enjoy them." Chess teaches you that winning and losing is part of the game. The emphasis is you and your career experiences. How you evaluate them and how you can use them to be a better person is what is important. Not how many toys you have.

The fourth mistake is seeing life with a fixed mindset. A fixed mindset is the opposite of the American Dream. The fixed mindset says that because of who you are and where you come from, that is the prime mover of failure or success, no matter how hard you work. Research does not prove this. It proves just the opposite.

You may idolize your boss and think you'll never be like that. True, he may have a set of skills which you do not currently possess, but it doesn't mean you can't become as skilled as him or her. Your focus is effort and effort alone, not talent, not circumstance, not your weight, not your big nose, etc.

Effort, hope, patience, self-forgiveness and optimism are now your guidelines.

Relationships

We live in a world of relationships in both life and career. You have four simultaneous identities as careerist: Boss (eventually), subordinate, peer and competitor.

It's complicated. Relating this to chess, there are many pieces on the board. They are all on the move. Who is doing what to whom? What is your next move? How will it affect this or that relationship?

Relationships for the purpose of your career can be classified into two broad categories: *allies and competitors* or another way of putting it, *supporters and detractors*. Your existence in the context of relationships should be one, creating allies and supporters and two, recognizing competitors and detractors. You also have a neutral group to keep your eye on. Allies or competitors might appear from here.

These classifications apply inside and outside organizations. Companies are competing for market share, and you are competing for you bosses attention and other needs that you have from other departments within the company.

In addition to creating allies and supporters, you should strive to make current players better allies and better supporters. Using chess as a metaphor, the principles, "Don't move the same piece twice," and "develop Knights before Bishops," are examples. In the opening your pieces aren't doing you much good. So how do you make them better allies? Develop them. Note the word "them." By moving the same piece twice, you weaken both the piece moved and the others that you have left in place. The piece that you moved twice is out on his own with no help, and the other pieces remain ineffective by their remaining idle. On the piece moved, there is now a lot of pressure to perform, and perhaps it is too much pressure.

110

Think about your people if you are a manager or supervisor. Are you doing the same thing with them? Are one of your "pawns" about to be promoted?

Summary

One could write an entire book of metaphors about chess and careers. Here I have given you just a few. But the point is that chess helps your brain deal with complicated relationships, and dealing with complicated relationships is what your career is all about, even the relationship with yourself.

Chapter Eight: Chess and Jr. Golf

Sometime before I retired to Florida, I began to think about the scope of golf like I thought about the scope of chess. I know how vast chess is and why no two games are alike. Surely there must be similar numbers in golf.

I started thinking about how big a golf course is vs. how small a golf ball is. I wondered how many possible lies there are on an average course. I figured it out by estimating that the average landing surface of a golf course is 60 acres. So if you were to play a course enough times, how many games would it take for you to cover the entire course? That is, hit every possible place that the ball could land? That's one question. The other is in what order? Well, it's 7.2 followed by 70 zeros! 7.2 trevigintiilion. For humans, it may as well be infinity, and that is why no two golf games are alike. Just like chess. Could it be that the same principles that govern better chess apply to golf?

Golf employs strategic thinking too, just like chess. In chess, you observe, think, plan, focus, *move,* then evaluate. In golf you observe, think, plan, focus, *hit,* then evaluate. Notice that the actual activity of both games is only one of 6 separate elements. I got better at golf when incorporated into my practice mentality, everything else but the "hit" part, and I focused on the rest: think better, plan better, focus better, and evaluate better. I was amazed.

113

Chess Camp

When I got to Florida, I observed Jr. Golf in person for the first time. It was the summer and it was hot. The kids got there at 8:30 a.m., and were outside doing golf drills until 11:30 a.m., and by the time they got to go inside they were hot and drenched. The thought struck me that adding chess would fit right into this program. It would employ the same type of thinking that helps a kid's golf game, plus it would give them a break from the heat.

Although adding chess to Jr. Golf was a novel idea, teaching chess to kids didn't come from out of the blue. In the later part of my career at age 52, our internet startup had just run out of funding and my 125,000 shares of stock disappeared along with the company. I decided to take a break from my career pursuits and get an MBA, so I went back to school full time. Cal State University at San Francisco had a program for working adults, where all classes were held 9 a.m. to 5 p.m. on Saturday and Sunday.[14] During the week, I studied 5 hours a day and filled the rest of my time experimenting with part-time work in totally unrelated fields. I took one job as a tutor/instructor at Lindamood Bell, teaching reading to illiterate adults and kids who were having trouble learning to read[ii]. For job number two, I became a chess instructor at the Berkely

---

[14] For two friggin' years!

Chess Academy in Berkely California where I learned how to teach chess to kids.

I really liked it and went out on my own and founded the *Sausalito Chess Academy,* creating after school programs for various elementary schools in Marin County. I ended up with 8 after school programs and about 15 kids each, for a total of 120 kids.

I got my MBA, using the Sausalito Chess Academy as the basis of my thesis. Good things come to an end and I continued my career after I moved away from the Bay Area and disbanded the Sausalito Chess Academy. I went on with my life, playing chess online daily and playing golf when I could fit it into my work schedule.

Fast forward to retirement and living in Florida, I approached Ben Herring, the club pro who ran the Jr. Golf Program at the Golf Club at Venetian Bay, my neighborhood club of which I am a member. It took some convincing, and Ben with a skeptical eye, gave me 1 hour out of 3 days to present chess to the kids and have them play. That was 3 years ago. We now have chess every day of golf camp where the kids learn chess the right way, and it gets them out of the hot sun sooner. The kids love it and the parents love it. There couldn't be a better combination of complementary learning platforms for kids.

Chess Camp & Jr. Golf at the Venetian Bay Golf Club

Playing Chess v. Playing Golf

Golf and chess are more like real life, where you have a lot of time between the action. Since I play a lot of golf, I started wondering about golf the same way I did chess. Just like chess, no two golf games are alike.

An interesting concept is to look at the "empty time," and "waiting time," involved in golf. *Empty Time* is the time when you are not actively playing. *Waiting Time* is the time between shots when you are playing or practicing. If you know how to use empty time and waiting time correctly, you have a huge advantage. In golf, there are 3 critical waiting times:

✓ One: the time between shots, when you are playing the game.

✓ Two: Practice time, of course; and

✓ Three: the time between games.

In golf (or any competitive hobby or pastime), there is pleasurable anticipation when thinking about the next time you will play. Most people do not relate this as being part of the game, but it is. Golfers are fond of saying "it's all in your head." Taking this seriously, I picked up a book called, "Golf State of Mind," by David Mackenzie. As I read through this remarkable book, which does indeed alter your state of mind regarding golf, my scores improved. The paradox being you don't work on or even think about your score. Your focus is everything but. The discussion sounded strangely familiar, and when he used the word "mindset," my mind went, "AHA!" And then he referred to "Mindset, the New Psychology of Success," by Dr. Carol Dweck. Well, whadaya know! The principles that apply to chess apply to golf too!

I started thinking about my life in sports. I was always good at "instinct sports." Sports that are so fast you don't have time to think. In baseball, think about being at bat. For example, you don't have time to evaluate a 90 mile an hour fast ball. The same with football, surfing, snowboarding, tennis, racquetball, etc. Wining at instinct sports can be very satisfying because they mostly aren't like real life. To me, this is why they are fun and such a diversion. It's like living a fantasy. But now, as I enjoy my retirement years, chess and golf along with writing, have become my primary pastimes.

Summary

Chess and golf have many benefits. They help families develop relationships. They help parents keep channels of communication open, and they add a lot of fun to holiday get togethers. For information on chess camps go to www.venetianbaychess.org.

Epilogue

I've had three passions in my life: chess, surfing and golf, in that order. Chess, I took up at age 8, surfing at age 14, and golf at age 35. All 3 are enduring and still with me.

Anyway, as a little kid playing chess, I just had fun playing it with no deep thoughts at all. It was only later in life when I learned to teach that I started studying the game and became fascinated with it. I often have mused if the qualities and skills that practicing chess create, can be quantified much like EQ has been quantified. That is, you can go online and take an EQ test and be evaluated for your "Emotional Quotient," just like IQ. Perhaps some curious individual will create a "CQ" test. I hope so.

When I was a late teen and had been surfing for a few years, I recall sitting outside[15] waiting for a wave on a beautiful day. I began pondering with awe, wonder and gratitude, all that the ocean was giving me. No two days were alike and no two waves were alike. It seemed miraculous to me and I felt like I was in the presence of God himself, and all I was doing was sitting on my board waiting for the next wave, which would be different from the wave before. And the next day I went surfing everything would be different again. I

---

[15] "Outside" to surfers is the place you sit on your board waiting for a wave. It's "outside" the break. The "break" is the area were all the waves break.

continued experiencing these sacred moments while surfing well into my fifties.

Golf strikes me in a powerful way, just like surfing does, but from a distinct perspective. Golf is learning the same way that chess is learning. Golf shots are trade-offs, and each shot is a lesson. Golf and chess explore the infinity of the mind, and at times this mental vista in your mind's eye dwarfs your actual vision of the real world. How can hitting a little white ball into a hole 400 yards away be so much fun? How can 64 squares and two sets of chessmen produce incomprehensible, awe-inspiring combinations?

So here I am in my seventies, on the golf course in the early morning. I find myself feeling the same way as I did years ago when I sat on my board on beautiful glassy mornings. Between shots I look around at the subtle grandeur surrounding me. I appreciate the variety of plants and animals, the fish jumping from various ponds, the occasional alligator cruising by, and the early morning shadows and rays of light at play in the forest next to the fairway. That same feeling of gratitude pours over me, and I conclude that gratitude is what it's all about.

Suggested Reading

On Chess:

How Not To Play Chess by Eugene Znosko-Borovsky

Logical Chess, Move by Move by Irving Chernev

Simple Checkmates by A.J. Gilliam

Thinking With Chess by Alexey W. Root

The Art of Sacrifice in Chess by Rudolf Spielmann

The Moves That Matter by Jonathan Rowson

On Life:

Atomic Habits by James Clear

Authentic Happiness by Martin E.P. Seligman

Flourish by Martin E.P. Seligman

Grit by Angela Duckworth

How to Fail at Everything and Still Win Big by Scott Adams

How Children Succeed/Grit, Curiosity and the Hidden Power of Character by Paul Tough

Learned Optimism by Martin E.P. Seligman

Let My People Go Surfing by Yvon Chouinard

Mindset by Carol Dweck

The Art of Learning by Josh Waitzkin

The Artist's Way by Julia Cameron

Transformed! The Science of Spectacular Living by Drs. Judith & Bob Wright

Reframing Your Brain by Scott Adams

Working Identity by Herminia Ibarra

Sources & References

Online:

Chess.com

Chess.com: Why Superbowl QB Joe Burrow Plays Chess. Updated Feb. 22, 2022.

Chessdelta.com

Commonswikimedia.com

Image References:

Lady Howe Checkmates Ben Franklin: National Portrait Gallery. Edward Harrison. Oil on Canvas. 1867

The Chess Players by Thomas Eakins: MOMA. Oil on wood. 1867

Forleo, Marie, "Why Even Your Failures Are Just Opportunities to Learn." Presented by Tom Bilyeu. Retrieved from You Tube. https://youtu.be/kk5NTcwbdBE

Notated Chessboard: Kidschessworld.com

Acknowledgments

Thanks to Chess.com for creating a platform for playing chess with people worldwide and a repository of chess knowledge.

Many thanks to Ben Herring, GMM at the Golf Club at Venetian Bay for his enthusiastic support. And thanks to all my golfing buddies at the Club.

Thank you to two special people who have helped with this book.

My wife Barbara, who has read and re-read the manuscript and been at my side through it all.

Megan Werenski, the up and coming lady golf pro/business strategist, for your thoughts, comments and edits!

About the Author

Mr. Ashley started playing chess at age 8 on the streets in his hometown of Cohoes, NY. He discovered surfing after moving to Southern California at age 11 and started playing golf in his early thirties.

In high school and college, in addition to being an avid surfer, Brian was a 3-year varsity track high hurdler, all league wide receiver, played baseball as an All-Star in the Babe Ruth League, and was awarded a full-ride football college scholarship as a wide receiver. Brian has a B.A. in Psychology and an MBA.

He went on to a successful and creative career in fashion home textiles, working with Design, and marketing many new products, including the first set of black Barbie bedding.

In mid-career he founded The Sausalito Chess Academy, a chess school for kids, in Marin County California, and after retirement, he founded the Venetian Bay Chess Academy in New Smyrna Beach, Florida.

He has five remarkably successful children, eleven grandchildren and three great grandchildren. He is currently retired and lives with his wife Barbara and plays golf and chess.

Endnotes

---

[i] On Soccer: Balls have been used in every culture known, in some form or another. Some ancient games resembled soccer and some didn't. One drawback that I see here is that soccer doesn't promote peace. We don't see chess riots but we do see soccer riots. Not that I am against soccer.

[ii] At Lindamood Bell I was trained in *symbol and cognitive imagery* and how to teach it, the basis of which is visualization and verbalization and it is taught like this: Reading is taking a symbol, that is, a letter, that has a specific sound, showing it to a student on a flashcard. After that, letters are arranged into words, which is a higher level meta-image. We then take words with their visual and sound imagery, then combine those words creating even bigger meta-images called paragraphs which is an even higher combination of images and sounds, and so on until you were in the realm of books of ideas, all visualized in your mind's eye, complete with soundtrack! What non-readers couldn't remember before Lindamood Bell, after the program, they learned and remembered like aces.

NOTES: